the
mental
health mixtape

Holistic workbook and journal with activities to improve wellness and alleviate depression and anxiety – for Black men who want to do the work

Lady in your life? Check out our other workbooks for Black women

SELF CARE WORKBOOK FOR BLACK WOMEN
A 150+ page activity book covering mental, physical, spiritual and emotional self help practices. Complete with a 12-month planner and guided journal

SPIRITUAL SELF CARE FOR BLACK WOMEN
A guided journal and 12-month planner with more in-depth self reflection and spirituality activities

EMOTIONAL SELF CARE FOR BLACK WOMEN
A self help activity book and guided journal to specifically address the thoughts, beliefs and triggers which affect your emotions and behavior

PRAYER JOURNAL FOR BLACK WOMEN
52 Week Devotional with bible verses, gratitude checklists, lessons from God, prayers for others

**Stress Less Press are a Black-owned independent publisher.
If you enjoy this book, please consider supporting us by leaving a review on Amazon!**

the table of contents

introduction

stigma

Do you relate to any of these thoughts, feelings or assumptions about mental health and seeking help for mental health struggles?

I feel pressure to always be 'strong'

I don't want other people knowing my business

Admitting there's a problem will make me less of a man

I worry my problems won't be taken seriously if I seek help

I worry about expressing my emotions or venting my frustrations, and being seen as 'aggressive' or 'crazy'

No one understands my problems

I don't want to be a burden

I feel like mental health services don't cater to my unique needs and experiences as a Black man

Research shows that Black men are particularly concerned about mental health stigma and often suffer in silence because of it. The pressure to conform to traditional gender norms such a toughness, fearlessness, and invulnerability means they are less likely to open up or seek professional help for mental health struggles. Many men aren't taught how to process and express their emotions, leading to a sense of isolation, anger, and resentment. With these emotions brewing inside and no outlet to process them, for some men it comes out in aggression or even violence.

For those that do try to seek help and appropriate outlets, there are barriers that prevent Black men in particular from accessing support. This includes the cultural incompetency of mental health care providers and the underrepresentation of Black providers who are known to give more appropriate and effective care. According to research, Black Americans are 20% more likely to experience serious mental health problems than the general population yet Black men are less likely to be offered therapy when we actually seek help.

the harsh truth

Research suggests that men who struggle to speak openly about their emotions are less able to recognize symptoms of mental health problems in themselves, and are therefore less likely to receive support. To cope with their untreated problems, men are also more likely to use harmful coping methods such as drugs or alcohol.

Long-term untreated mental health problems are a huge contributor to the high rates of suicide we see amongst Black men. This is attributed to socioeconomic hardship (due to systemic inequalities), lack of social support (due to mental health stigma), contact with the criminal justice system and of course, racism and discrimination.

We know that racism is wide-reaching and it shows up in so many different forms including personal, cultural, structural and institutional racism. Because of this, it's been shown to result in a profound feeling of pain, harm and humiliation, often leading to despair and exclusion - or in other words, mental health problems. This on the backdrop of historical trauma and violence experienced by Black men in America, creates layers of individual and cultural trauma that is difficult to manage, and therefore puts us at higher risk for poor mental health.

There are many different signs and symptoms of mental health problems, all of which can impact an individual at different levels including:
- Emotional: sadness, anger, anxiety, irritation, low confidence and self-esteem and lack of motivation
- Mental: negative thoughts and racing thoughts
- Physical and physiological: lack of sleep, digestion, racing heartbeat, raised blood pressure, muscle tension, headaches, tiredness and dizziness
- Social: lack of enjoyment and social disengagement

Some symptoms are more often associated with certain diagnosis, for example, extreme low mood is a sign of depression but can also be present in other diagnosis. Others such as feeling anxious may persist across all diagnosis. Hearing voices, hallucinations and delusions tend to be associated with psychotic disorders. An individual may be affected to the point that they are unable to deal with everyday strains and stresses and to continue with normal routines. If you are experiencing any of these symptoms, consult a mental health professional immediately. You can find a list of resources on p.75.

what mental health means to me

Let's start with where you're at with your mental health. How is your mental health overall? Have you struggled in the past? What does good mental health look like to you?

_____

_____

_____

_____

_____

_____

_____

_____

_____

_____

_____

_____

_____

_____

_____

_____

_____

_____

_____

_____

_____

_____

_____

_____

_____

mental health
assessment

Complete the questionnaire below. Think about your behaviors over the past 14 days. Any questions you answer 'never' or 'rarely' to might be something to focus on in the future

1 = Never   2 = Rarely   3 = Sometimes   4 = Often

	1	2	3	4
I have focused on the things I can control				
I have taken time for personal reflection (e.g. journalling)				
I have taken a break from social media (2+ hours)				
I have attended a counselling / therapy session				
I have asked for help if I needed it				
I have challenged my negative thoughts				
I have taken time to be alone				
I have set boundaries with others				
I have avoided situations that will trigger me				
I have connected with friends and/or family				

things to remember

If this book is your first time actively working on your inner self, there are a few things you should keep in mind

- Sometimes you're not going to enjoy reading this book. Similar to going to the gym, you go because you know it's good for you and you know you'll likely feel way better afterwards. The 'during' part can be uncomfortable, but it's worth doing the work as it's bound to pay off over time

- Your experience working through this book may not be filled with epiphanies and breakthroughs like we see in the movies. More like small incremental steps towards a deeper understanding of yourself. Be patient. Results aren't always immediate

- Even if you don't feel like you're struggling mentally at the moment, this book can still be valuable. Think of it as an act of self care that will arm you with the tools to deal with challenges if/when they arise in the future. Prevention is always better than cure

- To get the most out of the book, complete the activities in a place where you feel relaxed and free of distractions

- You might have been raised in an environment where feelings were swept under the carpet, you were told to 'man up', or that 'boys don't cry'. You might not have been given many opportunities to be safely vulnerable, or perhaps you had no choice but to be strong. As a result, it might feel incredibly difficult to get vulnerable on these pages now. That's completely understandable, but try to remember that this book is a safe space to explore your feelings in order to process them. No judgement here

- Use this book as a stepping stone. If you finish the book and feel as though you've just scratched the surface then it's a great idea to find a qualified person you can talk to. Use the themes that you uncover during the completion of this book and address it with a therapist. You can find mental health resources on p.75

chapter one:
knowing

This chapter will help you to illuminate who you are as a person, your strengths and areas to improve. It will give you the tools to recognize behaviors within yourself and build your self awareness so you can continue to grow

value yourself

Understanding your values will help you recognize areas of your life that need more attention. Rank the values on the left from 1-10, with 1 being the most important. Rate how successfully you currently live true to these on a scale of 1-10, with 1 being very successfully. Remember, there's no right or wrong answer here. These are your personal values and no one else's

		IMPORTANCE	SUCCESS
love	Do you prioritize finding/maintaining a romantic connection?		
money	Is money the main driver in your life?		
friends & family	Does spending time with your friends/family make you the happiest?		
success	Are your achievements what define you?		
faith	Does your religion or sense of spirituality ground you the most?		
knowledge	Does learning new things give you a sense of purpose?		
adventure	Do new experiences make you feel alive?		
respect	Does giving and receiving respect affirm your sense of self?		
independence	Is being self-sufficient a big part of your identity?		
fairness	Do you seek fairness in the world and in your relationships?		
creativity	Is creative expression what makes you feel alive?		
loyalty	Do you pride yourself on your loyalty to others?		

reflection

Use this space to ask yourself: How do I ensure my life choices align with my values? What causes me to stray from living to my values? Are there any other values you'd like to focus on in your life?

life balance: connection

You may notice that when you feel stressed or low, you withdraw from others. To create balance and maintain our wellbeing, it's important that we strive for personal connection each day. Use the space below to create a spider diagram detailing what you currently do (or would like to do more of) to fulfil the 'connection' part of your life. Answer the question in centre for a deeper dive

E.g. family, friends, community.
What sort of relationships do you want to build? How do you want to be in these relationships?

life balance:
achievement

It's very important to accomplish things every day, whether it be small tasks or bigger goals - especially when we feel low. Create a spider diagram of what you'd like to achieve (career and otherwise) and what you can do daily to give you a sense of achievement. Answer the question in centre for a deeper dive

E.g. work, chores, study.
Do you feel pressure as a Black man to overachieve to counteract negative stereotypes?

life balance: enjoyment

When we're struggling emotionally, or even just focused on the daily grind, we sometimes stop doing the things we enjoy. Create a spider diagram as a reminder of activities you enjoy and think about ways you can carve out more time for them daily. Answer the question in centre for a deeper dive

E.g. hobbies and fun. Are there any new hobbies you'd like to make time for? (explore your hobbies further on p.58)

thinking or feeling

It's helpful to differentiate thoughts and feelings. Thoughts are opinions or assumptions, and are often a result of how we feel. Alternatively, feelings can be a product of what we're thinking. Read the statements below and see if you can discern the difference between the two

	THOUGHT	FEELING
I feel lonely	☐	☐
I feel down	☐	☐
I feel that something bad is going to happen	☐	☐
I feel angry	☐	☐
I feel like I'll never amount to anything	☐	☐
I feel broken	☐	☐
I feel stupid	☐	☐
I feel like a burden	☐	☐
I feel like nothing ever goes right for me	☐	☐
I feel like life will never get better	☐	☐
I feel scared	☐	☐

Do you ever label your thoughts as feelings? For example, 'I feel stupid' is actually a thought, but labelling it as a feeling means we accept it as a reality without requiring evidence. Rather than feeling stupid, the feeling deep down may be shame, sadness, or hurt. Use the feelings wheel on the next page to explore the language around feelings which can help us understand them more

date:

in your feelings

Have you ever struggled to put words to how you feel? Developing emotional vocabulary actually helps us to reduce negative emotions and experiences because it re-engages the rational mind. Adapted from the Dr. Gloria Willcox model, the feelings wheel below might help you to find the words to better communicate how you feel. If you can think of any other feelings, write them around the wheel

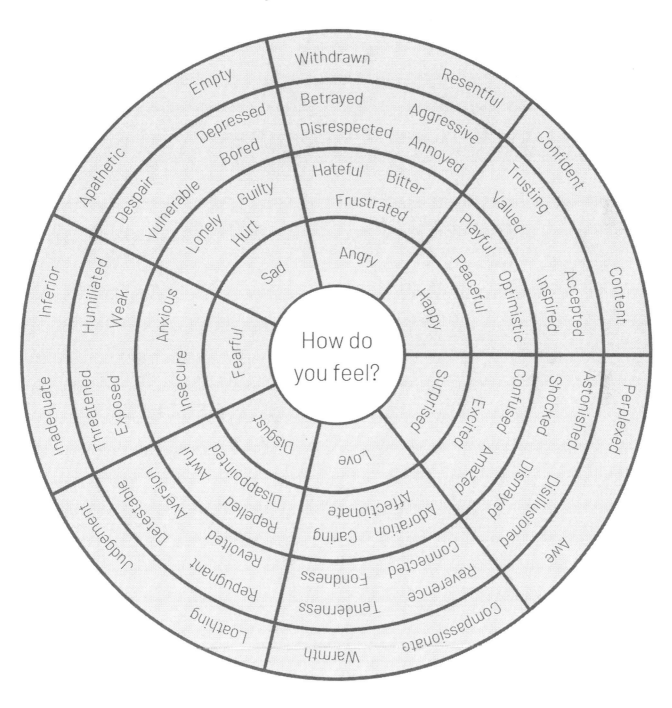

date:

b o d y   s c a n

Recognizing how our body feels can help us to identify our emotions and then work out how to deal with them. Using the checklists below, turn your attention to various parts of your body to help identify which emotion(s) you are feeling

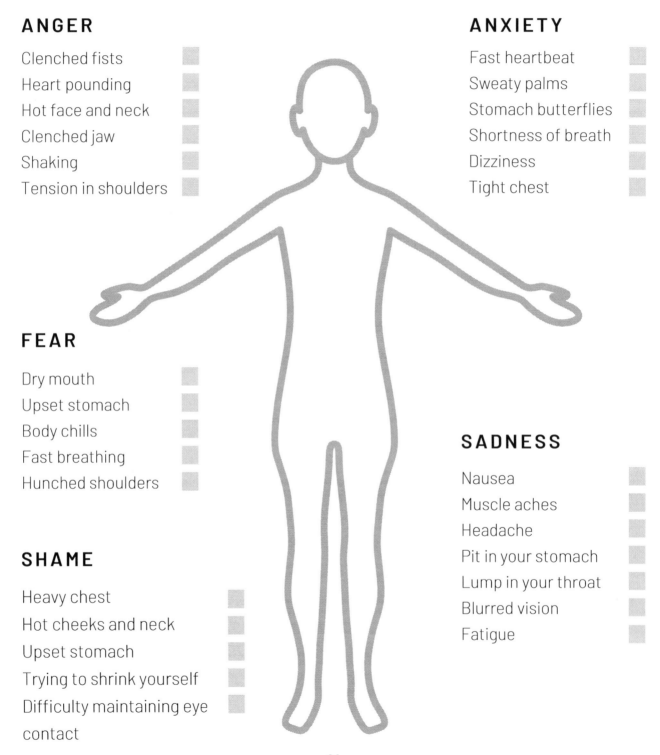

ANGER

Clenched fists ☐
Heart pounding ☐
Hot face and neck ☐
Clenched jaw ☐
Shaking ☐
Tension in shoulders ☐

ANXIETY

Fast heartbeat ☐
Sweaty palms ☐
Stomach butterflies ☐
Shortness of breath ☐
Dizziness ☐
Tight chest ☐

FEAR

Dry mouth ☐
Upset stomach ☐
Body chills ☐
Fast breathing ☐
Hunched shoulders ☐

SADNESS

Nausea ☐
Muscle aches ☐
Headache ☐
Pit in your stomach ☐
Lump in your throat ☐
Blurred vision ☐
Fatigue ☐

SHAME

Heavy chest ☐
Hot cheeks and neck ☐
Upset stomach ☐
Trying to shrink yourself ☐
Difficulty maintaining eye contact ☐

date:

day one

Use the previous exercises to reflect on your feelings for the day. The feelings wheel might help you put words to your feelings. Start out with a basic emotion in the centre of the wheel, then move outward until you have the best word(s) that fit the bill - pick up to 3. Remember feelings aren't 'good' or 'bad', they simply are what they are

How do you feel?

Why?

date:

day two

Use the previous exercises to reflect on your feelings for the day. The feelings wheel might help you put words to your feelings. Start out with a basic emotion in the centre of the diagram, then move outward until you have the best word(s) that fit the bill - pick up to 3. Remember feelings aren't 'good' or 'bad', they simply are what they are

How do you feel?

Why?

date:

day three

Use the previous exercises to reflect on your feelings for the day. The feelings wheel might help you put words to your feelings. Start out with a basic emotion in the centre of the diagram, then move outward until you have the best word(s) that fit the bill - pick up to 3. Remember feelings aren't 'good' or 'bad', they simply are what they are

How do you feel? _____

Why? _____

_____

_____

_____

_____

_____

_____

_____

_____

_____

_____

_____

_____

_____

_____

_____

_____

_____

_____

_____

_____

_____

_____

_____

date:

day four

Use the previous exercises to reflect on your feelings for the day. The feelings wheel might help you put words to your feelings. Start out with a basic emotion in the centre of the diagram, then move outward until you have the best word(s) that fit the bill - pick up to 3. Remember feelings aren't 'good' or 'bad', they simply are what they are

How do you feel? _____

Why? _____

_____

_____

_____

_____

_____

_____

_____

_____

_____

_____

_____

_____

_____

_____

_____

_____

_____

_____

_____

_____

_____

_____

_____

_____

_____

_____

date:

day five

Use the previous exercises to reflect on your feelings for the day. The feelings wheel might help you put words to your feelings. Start out with a basic emotion in the centre of the diagram, then move outward until you have the best word(s) that fit the bill - pick up to 3. Remember feelings aren't 'good' or 'bad', they simply are what they are

How do you feel?

Why?

date:

day six

Use the previous exercises to reflect on your feelings for the day. The feelings wheel might help you put words to your feelings. Start out with a basic emotion in the centre of the diagram, then move outward until you have the best word(s) that fit the bill - pick up to 3. Remember feelings aren't 'good' or 'bad', they simply are what they are

How do you feel? _____

Why? _____

_____

_____

_____

_____

_____

_____

_____

_____

_____

_____

_____

_____

_____

_____

_____

_____

_____

_____

_____

_____

_____

_____

_____

_____

date:

day seven

Use the previous exercises to reflect on your feelings for the day. The feelings wheel might help you put words to your feelings. Start out with a basic emotion in the centre of the diagram, then move outward until you have the best word(s) that fit the bill - pick up to 3. Remember feelings aren't 'good' or 'bad', they simply are what they are

How do you feel? _____

Why? _____

_____
_____
_____
_____
_____
_____
_____
_____
_____
_____
_____
_____
_____
_____
_____
_____
_____
_____
_____
_____
_____
_____
_____

chapter two:
learning & unlearning

In this chapter you'll find reflective exercises to help you to further explore how you feel and why. You'll learn about different ways of thinking and behaving and how to unlearn unhelpful ones

date:

triggered

In the previous chapter, when doing the 7-day diary, you may have been struggling to answer the 'why'. Why do you feel the way you do? Identifying your triggers can help with this. Let's start by understanding what triggers are

A trigger is something that brings undesirable emotions to the surface. Both internal (thoughts, feelings, memories) or external (people, places and situations) can cause these undesirable emotions to arise . You may associate being 'triggered' with PTSD (post traumatic stress disorder) after someone has experienced an extremely traumatic event such as military conflict, assault or the loss of a loved one. However, you can be triggered by many things, even if you haven't been through something you'd consider as being 'traumatic'.

Have any of these internal or external triggers occurred recently?

you felt rejected	you felt betrayed
you were discriminated against	you were excluded from something
you felt a loss of conrol	you felt insecure
you were visiting somewhere from your past	an interaction with someone from your past
you had too much to do and felt overwhelmed	you experienced financial problems

date:

trigger warning

Go back and read through your 7-day diary. Are there any themes you can spot? If not, pay attention to your feelings over the next few weeks and everytime you feel an undesirable emotion arise, think about what lead to it

PEOPLE

PLACES

SITUATIONS

THOUGHTS/FEELINGS

date:

get to the root

Now you've identified what triggers you, let's dig deeper. Follow the feelings back to their origins by picking one of the triggers and making sense of how it relates to your current feelings

What happened? Write the facts of what happened (who, what, when, where). Once you've finished, reread the entry and annotate with words to describe your thoughts and feelings

digging deeper

We'll now explore the experience further. If you're exploring painful memories in this exercise, take your time and remember that addressing these past experiences will help your emotional wellbeing in the long run

What was the worst part?

Write about the worst moments of the experience and how it made you feel. Try to be detailed if you can. Once you've finished, re-read the entry and annotate with words to describe the senses you felt in your body (tension, nausea, lightheaded etc)

building strength

A silver living of trauma is that the healing process presents opportunities to build strength and grow. This could be through deepened relationships with others, new outlooks on life, gratitude and appreciation of life, or even spirituality. Answer the below questions to reflect on this

Write 5 personal strengths you had before this experience

1. _____
2. _____
3. _____
4. _____
5. _____

Which of your strengths in particular helped you get through the experience?

_____
_____
_____
_____
_____
_____

What new personal strengths have you developed because of the experience?

_____
_____
_____
_____
_____
_____

take a breath

This exercise is a great way to practice relaxation and mindfulness. It's a tool you can use when you need to calm down, especially if you've been triggered. It may be difficult to fully relax at first (this is perfectly normal). The key is to keep practicing so you can lean on this technique when you need it the most

step 1: Find a quiet, comfortable place. This could be your car, your bedroom or anywhere else you're free from distractions

step 2: Close your eyes and try to transport your mind to your favorite place, doing your favorite thing. Somewhere you feel safe and happy

step 3: Clench your fists for about 4 seconds then let it go. Exhale for 4 seconds as you unclench. Repeat this 2-3 times then move onto the next step

step 4: Next, tighten your shoulders for 4, then relax for 4. Remember the deep breathing from the previous step

step 5: Now do the same with your stomach muscles

step 6: Repeat this throughout your entire body starting from your head to your toes. It should take about 10 minutes. If there are any areas you can't clench, just focus on how each body part feels whilst doing your deep breathing. For example, your ears: can you hear your breath? As you get practice this exercise more, you'll learn to relax the whole body at once

step 7: If you notice your thoughts drifting back to whatever situation has made you angry or anxious, that's ok. Try to redirect your attention back to how your body feels and focus on breathing. This will take some practice

reflection

Use this space to reflect on your experience of 'taking a breath' or mindful breathing. Did it work for you and why?

buy some time

When you feel your emotions rising, delaying your reaction can make all the difference. Below are some tips for buying time so you're able to deal with the situation calmly and constructively

- Count to ten. Yes, we know it's cliché but taking a few mindful breaths really can save you when things go south

- Remove yourself. If you find yourself in a situation that causes undesirable emotions to build up inside you, start to make an exit plan - just in case

- Use your imagination. Imagine what your calmest friend would say to you in that moment and give yourself the same advice

- Use your imagination some more. Transport yourself to the most relaxing and serene place you can imagine. Think about how you would feel if you were there

- Shout it out. Shout at the top of your lungs (maybe in a pillow so not to disturb people in your vacinity!)

- Distract yourself. Occupy yourself by doing something you enjoy. Physical activity like going for a walk or going to the gym works great for this

- Get creative. This could be writing in a journal, doodling or painting. Basically, anything that will redirect your energy into something besides the situation at hand

- Reach out to your support system. Whether it be a family member or a close friend, find someone to offload to. Ideally, you want to speak to someone removed from the situation so they can give you some perspective

- Remember, it's never too late to take a deep breath and choose to express your feelings differently. Give rational thinking time to kick in

reflection

Use this space to reflect on your experience of 'buying some time'. Did it work for you and why? Also reflect on the event that lead to you needing to buy some time

cool off

Now you've learned the skills to effectively identify and manage your emotions, try putting them into practice. The next time you think you've been triggered (and when you're no longer feeling angry or emotional), reflect on the questions below

What happened?   What was the trigger? Describe it below and explain how it came about

What do you feel?   Did you notice a change in your body? What sensations did you feel? Where did your mind go? Write this down

What next?   What were the consequences of your actions as a result of your heightened emotions? What can you do you stay in control of the situation next time? Write your action plan below

let's talk

In the previous chapter you identified your feelings, now let's work on communicating them - either to the people in your inner circle, HR or to a professional. Talking about your feelings can be daunting if you're not used to it, but it's an essential part of taking charge of your wellbeing. Here are some tips

- Start by understanding your 'why'. When you open up to someone, what outcome are you hoping for? Are you seeking support? Do you just want to be heard, or do you want to let go of the struggle you've been carrying by yourself? Knowing your why will allow you to suggest things that person can do to help

- Do what feels comfortable to you. There's no pressure to have a face-to-face conversation if you feel uncomfortable with this. Find a method that suits you, whether it's sending a text, an email, or even writing a letter

- Prepare. You likely have hopes for how the person will react to you opening up, but don't be discouraged if you're met with shock, awkwardness or dismissiveness. Due to the stigma associated with mental health, the person may not know how to handle this new information, and as a result may say things like "you've just got the blues", "man up" or "pull yourself together". Try not to take it personally

- But try not to overthink it. It might help to have some key points in mind that you'd like to cover, some phrases on hand such as "I've been finding it hard to cope recently", or even some online resources you can share that you feel sums things up perfectly, but don't get too in your head about everything. This likely won't be your first and last time discussing these issues. The main thing is to be open and honest about your feelings and experiences

- It will be so worth it. While it may feel unthinkable to open up about your struggles, the alternative is likely even more intolerable. Dealing with this alone means you're missing out on invaluable support that will help you to overcome your struggles. In the process, you might even find that the person you open up to has a similar experience, which will help you feel less alone

keep it 100

Imagine you have the freedom to open up to your closest confidant. What would you say?
Use the space below to write to this person, expressing the struggles and everything else
you've been holding in. This is a safe space, so be as authentic as you can

New message	— ⤢ ✕
To	
Subject	

Send 📎 | +   🗑 | +

negative thoughts

Negative thoughts are part of a vicious cycle we can find ourselves in when we feel low. When we repeat these self-critical thoughts to ourselves, we begin to accept them as fact. Common examples of negative thoughts include: "I'm worthless" "I'm a failure" "I'm lazy and irresponsible". Write below negative thoughts you have about yourself

negative thinking styles

In this exercise, we'll identify unhelpful thinking styles you may have adopted. Do any of your negative thoughts fall into the below unhelpful thinking styles? Tick the ones that apply

Catastrophising: Thinking things are much worse than they are or obsessing over the worst case scenario. E.g. if you make a small mistake at work, you'll immediately worry you'll be fired

Overgeneralizing: Applying one negative experience to all other experiences. E.g. if something on your to-do list hasn't been completed you may think "I've achieved nothing, today has been pointless"

Ignoring the positive: Focusing your thinking on bad events and overlooking good events. E.g. after the game you just think about that one missed shot and not the rest of the game played well

Self blame and mind reading: Finding a way to blame yourself if anything goes wrong, even if it has nothing to do with you. E.g. a friend is short with you and your immediate thought is that you've done something to upset them

Labeling: Similar to overgeneralizing, labeling is taking one characteristic of ourselves and applying it to our entire being. E.g. because I failed a test so I am a failure. This also tends to bleed into how we view others. E.g. because a colleague was late to work, they are irresponsible.

Minimizing/maximizing: Maximizing your failures and minimizing your successes. Positive events carry less weight than negative ones. E.g. even though you hit a home run earlier in the game, I let my team down when I struck out later in the game

Blaming: In a conflict, you focus on the other person as a source of the problem and ignore the role you may have played in it. You expect the other person to change or fix things when there are things you could do

date:

challenging my negative thoughts

Negative thoughts are normal, but it's important to challenge them so they don't stick. Now we've begun to recognize negative thoughts and styles, we'll develop some strategies to challenge these thoughts. Ask yourself the questions below to interrogate how logical this thinking is

What is the
negative
thought?

What evidence
do you have to
support this
thought?

What evidence
do you have
against this
thought?

What might you
say to a friend
who expressed
this thought?

Does this
negative thought
motivate you to
change?

If this thought is
truc, what is the
worst case
scenario?

37

switch it up

When bad things happen to us in our past, we can resort to having a set view of ourself and the world. Here are some common thoughts that are unhelpful and their alternatives

UNHELPFUL THOUGHTS	VS	HELPFUL THOUGHTS
what happened was my fault		what happened wasn't my fault
i should have done something different		i did my best in a hard situation
what happened means something bad about me		what happened isn't a reflection of me
i can't trust anyone		i can trust others
i'm ashamed about what happened		i don't need to feel guilt or shame
this is likely to happen again in the future		i have control over my future
i deserved it		i didn't deserve it

realistic self talk

We've explored ways to challenge our negative self talk, now let's put it into practice. In this exercise we'll find ways to stifle your inner judge, helping to boost confidence and resilience. Fill this in as and when you're faced with challenges to help you counteract negative self-talk. Also pay attention to any patterns that emerge in what triggers your negative self-talk

SITUATION	NEGATIVE SELF TALK	REALISTIC SELF TALK
Speaking to someone new	I'll make a fool of myself	I'm a good person with lots to offer. I can't control what other people think of me
A project didn't go as planned	I'm such an idiot! I screwed up and I'll never live this down	I tried my best. I can learn from this and I know I'll do better next time

realistic self talk

SITUATION	NEGATIVE SELF TALK	REALISTIC SELF TALK

affirmations

Now that we've unpacked your negative thoughts, let's write some affirmations. We all need a reminder sometimes, so refer to this page whenever the negative thoughts start to get loud. Some examples might include: "I am worth it" "I am loved" "I have what it takes to succeed"

attitude of gratitude

You may still be struggling with counter arguments for your negative thoughts. Bringing positive thinking into your daily life does take practice, but it can help your wellbeing in a number of ways, including improving your relationships, reducing anger, increasing empathy and forgiveness of yourself and others. One way we can build a positive mentality is through gratitude. While gratitude can't make injustice, loss or pain disappear, what it can do is give us hope. Here are some tips to live a life of gratitude

Simple acts of kindness: Kindness and gratitude go hand in hand because when we're aware we're doing something nice for someone else, we feel good about ourselves *and* others. You can put it into practice straight away, and you'll start to get those feel-good hormones pumping immediately! Doing a small gesture daily like shooting a friend a thoughtful text or shovelling snow from an elderly neighbor's driveway will make you feel helpful, optimistic and will boost your self-esteem.

Show gratitude to others: Making an effort to express genuine gratitude to both strangers and people in your life can go a long way in boosting your mental health. It starts a ripple effect and those people then want to spread the positive vibes to others. It might be as simple as saying 'thank you' to a service person and *really* meaning it, or it could be letting a friend or family member know you appreciate them. Now, that's not to say that communicating gratitude won't feel awkward at first, especially between Black men. We unfortunately do still live in a world where male intimacy is stigmatized. It's ok to feel hesitant about expressing appreciation to male friends for fear of being ridiculed. Do try to push through those feelings though, just to see how it feels. You could try it in small increments by starting off with an "I appreciate you, Bro" and work up to being more specific about why you appreciate the person and why the relationship is important to you.

Take note: You might already mentally take note of your blessings here and there, but starting or ending your day by physically writing them down makes them more concrete and real. It's also helpful for those who are struggling with their mental health because after a while of keeping gratitude journals, you're left with a great collection of inspiring material to look back on when you're feeling low.

Use the prompted gratitude journal pages on the next few pages to express what you're grateful for!

gratitude journal

Write about a person that helped you through a difficult time

gratitude journal

Write about the positive changes you've made in your life recently

date:

gratitude journal

Write about what you love about being a Black man

date:

gratitude journal

Write about something that makes you excited for the future

date:

gratitude journal

Who or what in your life do you find yourself taking for granted? Write about what you
appreciate the most about this person or thing

_____
_____
_____
_____
_____
_____
_____
_____
_____
_____
_____
_____
_____
_____
_____
_____
_____
_____
_____
_____
_____
_____
_____
_____
_____
_____
_____
_____
_____
_____

chapter three: doing

This chapter will provide self-help strategies you can try on your journey to healing and growing

problem solving

We've explored feelings a lot in this book so far, but you might be thinking, "what practical solutions can I actually put in place?". Don't worry, we got you, Bro! Here we'll cover effective problem solving processes so it's easier to move past your problems in the future

When we're feeling low, problems can easily pile up. This is because problem solving takes energy, energy that you're probably using just getting through the day. And that's ok. It's normal for everyday problems to take a backseat to a bigger problem, which is feeling better.

First thing's first, what's the problem? We have to identify the problem so we can find a solution. Think back to earlier in the book and use the feelings you uncovered to guide you. Be careful not to think of your feelings as the problem. For example, you might think, "the problem is that I am always stressed at work." when actually, the problems at work (such as difficulties with coworkers or a huge workload) are making you feel stressed.

You might find there are some big problems like "I have an eviction notice that comes up next week", some small problems like "I don't have time to hit the gym today" and then some problems in between.

Try to be specific here and make it clear what is going wrong and what you want to change. A good example would be "my best friend hasn't called me in a month" rather than "my relationships are mess" (remember negative thinking styles from earlier in the book? Yeah, this is what we call 'overgeneralizing'!)

What is the main problem you'd like to tackle and why?

problem solving

Now you've identified the problem, let's think of actions to solve it. To do this we'll write down three options for solving the problem and pick the best one. Now, this might sound overwhelming but we're not actually deciding on the best option just yet. It might be helpful to seek alternative perspectives from people you trust. This will allow you to see the problem in a way you hadn't considered. The main aim at this stage is to be thinking about *something* useful rather than letting the negative thoughts take over.

Here's an example to get you started:

The problem:

My colleague is racist. He's always making inappropriate comments which make me feel uncomfortable. I want to call him out but I'm worried i'll be called aggressive and my job will be at risk. It's making me anxious.

Possible actions:

OPTION 1: Just ignore him. I've dealt with racists in the past, and some people just aren't worth the energy

OPTION 2: Call him out and let him know that you won't stand for his comments anymore

OPTION 3: Read your staff handbook and see what the appropriate channels are to report this sort of behavior. Arrange to have a conversation with your boss about it, and put it in writing so you have a record of the incident

problem solving

Now it's your turn:

The problem:

_____

Possible actions:

_____

problem solving

Now we'll evaluate each option and decide which action is most likely to help the problem. We've provided an example for you here and you can complete your own evaluation on the next page

ACTION	PROS	CONS
Just ignore him	- By ignoring him you take away his power to get a rise out of you - Eventually he may just stop so the problem could resolve itself	- He may not stop but actually get worse instead - You may regret not doing anything to stop his behavior, which could cause a bigger internal struggle
Call him out	- He might begin to understand why his racist comments are unacceptable - Even if his behavior doesn't change, at least you've got it off your chest	- It could make the work environment awkward, possibly adding to your anxiety about the situation - He might respond aggressively to being confronted
Speak to your boss/HR	- Hopefully he'll be held accountable - This person's behavior is likely affecting your other colleagues, so addressing this issue will help others too	- The 'higher ups' may not take the issue seriously - Going this route will involve spending more time and energy (and paperwork!)

problem solving

Now it's your turn:

ACTION	PROS	CONS

problem solving

Now you've evaluated your options, look over the pros and cons for each option and decide which one is best (or which is least bad!). There are no hard and fast rules for making this decision; only that you actually make a decision. Take your time exploring the possibilities and once you've decided, it's time to move onto the next step: action.

The great thing about taking action is that even if you change your mind part way through and decide to go a different direction, at least you're still making progress towards finding a solution - it's a win-win.

There aren't many problems that you can solve completely with just one action. Solving a problem usually takes a few smaller actions. For example, if it's a financial problem you're having, your first action might be to gather your bank statements so you can assess everything, then you might create a budget. The process continues until you've reached the point of resolution. The point is to break the problem down into smaller chunks so you can get started - and try to be as specific and concrete as possible.

Write your action plan here:

self care

Is there anything you can do to keep life's problems at bay and your mental under control? The answer is: yes and no. The truth is, you can't completely eliminate hard times and mental struggles, but you can certainly make these instances less frequent and less severe - through self care

Self care is simply about tapping into what *you* specifically need to prosper and doing those things consistently. If hanging with a close friend weekly makes you feel good, keep doing it, especially when you're in a bad place. It's important that you don't give up self care when you need it the most, so try your best even if you don't feel like it. Here are some self care tips and how to prioritize when you're going through a difficult time:

Plan ahead. While it's not always the case, some stressful events can be predicted. Whether it's an upcoming review at work, a family event like Christmas, or maybe you're expecting a baby. You can increase your self care around these times to make you more resilient when you need to be.

Plan some more. Keeping dates in the diary really helps you stay on track with prioritizing self care as once you've committed it to iCal (or paper - no judgement here, Bro!) you're way more likely to follow through. It also helps you to have things to look forward to. Overall, it helps to think about the future rather than ruminate on the past. Whether it be a trip with friends or something small like a phone call with a loved one, write it down.

Always make time. Whether it's stealing a quick 15 minutes alone to reflect on your day, reading a book or meditating. Try to take time out of your day (every day) just for you, away from life's usual demands. Make sure it's things you actually enjoy, though - not things you 'think' you should be doing. So it could be listening to music, writing, working on art or even gaming. The main thing is to schedule it into your day so it becomes a natural part of your routine.

Ask for help and accept it. This one was mentioned earlier in the book, but it's worth repeating for the people in the back. Checking in with yourself, noticing when you're struggling, and reaching out is one of the best things you can do for your self care. No one expects you to deal with your stuff alone.

red flags

When we're in a bad place, we often indulge in 'red flag' behaviors. Being aware of these behaviors will help you to spot the signs before you spiral. Below are common behaviors people, especially men, engage in to cope. Tick the ones that apply

☐ Over-eating or under-eating

☐ Sitting around all day

☐ Overspending

☐ Keeping worries to yourself

☐ Lashing out at people

☐ Isolating yourself

☐ Acting impulsively

☐ More or less sex than normal

☐ Abusing alcohol or drugs

☐ Not resting

☐ Procrastinating

☐ Sleeping more or less than normal

Are there any other warning signs that you're struggling? Write them below

stay on track

Now you've identified red flag behaviors, what self care activities do you practice to avoid spiralling? Tick the ones that apply below. This checklist might also give you some ideas for ways to help yourself that you can implement straight away

☐ Eating regular balanced meals

☐ Getting enough sleep

☐ Keeping up with a daily routine

☐ Connecting with family & friends

☐ Making time for hobbies

☐ Reflecting on your feelings

☐ Exercising regularly

☐ Making time for relaxation

☐ Asking for help

☐ Challenging negative thoughts

☐ Being open with others

☐ Taking care of your responsibilities

Do you have any other behaviors that help you feel your best? List them below

black boy joy

Before we dive into what your hobbies are, let's first reflect on what joy means to you. Does joy mean you're at peace in life? Or is it about basking in your success? Use this space to define joy for yourself. You can also reflect on the most joyful moment in your life

discover your joy

What are your hobbies? If you're struggling to think of any, or you haven't made time for them in recent memory, you're not alone! Many adults on the path to getting grown stop trying new things that spark our interests simply because we're busy with raising families, working and sometimes life just gets in the way - but hobbies are so important to creating a balanced and fulfilled life. Let's figure out what your hobbies are

What were your hobbies as a child?

What activities do you currently enjoy in your life?

If you had a week's vacation, how would you ideally spend your time?

If money was no object, what would you do?

What is the one thing you could speak about all day and why?

things to try

Finding hobbies is usually a lot of trial and error. Create a list of hobbies you'd like to try out (we've provided some ideas to get you started) and tick them off as you go!

- Volunteering
- Learning a foreign language
- Photography
- Woodworking
- Taking cooking classes

keep it moving

Any well balanced self care routine should include regular exercise. Now this doesn't have to be grinding at the gym everyday or running marathons, but it's important to find sustainable workouts you can do regularly so you can reap the many benefits for your mental health. Here are some tips for developing an exercise program

Test your options. You might be the kind of guy that's strictly into running or swimming. On the other hand, weight training or calisthenics might be your bag. It's worth trying out a variety of things to see what suits your preferences. It's always a good idea to switch things up now and again, too.

Quantity over 'quality'. Now this might sound weird, but it's actually more important to exercise regularly (3 to 4 times a week) for shorter periods as opposed to super long sweat sessions that you only do once every few weeks. When you're struggling with your mental health, it may be hard to work up the motivation to do a strenuous workout, so even if it's just a brisk walk around the block, it's better than nothing.

Focus on your 'why'. Getting stacked is definitely a happy bi-product of exercising regularly, and the self-esteem boost is a great perk. However, seeing a change in the mirror shouldn't be your one and only goal. It'll take a while for you to start seeing physical results, so it's important to put an emphasis on the improvements in how feel rather than chasing after your dream body, so as to not get disheartened on your fitness journey - you're in it for the long haul!

Don't be too hard on yourself. When you're feeling especially low, it can be frustrating to be told "you just need to exercise to feel better". The truth is, exercise probably won't be a panacea for all of your mental health struggles. Sometimes it's just too hard to do, and that's ok. It's fine to focus on getting your mind right for a while. Beating yourself up about this will only make you feel worse.

Use the planner on the next page to schedule a month of exercises. You can use this month to find exercises that you truly enjoy so you're able to stick to a routine long-term. Don't go too hard though, it's a good idea to start small so you don't burn yourself out!

exercise planner

	WEEK 1	WEEK 2	WEEK 3	WEEK 4	WEEK 5
MON					
TUE					
WED					
THU					
FRI					
SAT					
SUN					

date:

reflection

What did you learn from your month of consistent exercise? How do you feel? Reflect on your experience here

fuel up

We know that proper nutrition does wonders for your mind and body, but it's not always easy to prioritize. Poor mental health often leads to poor diet - whether under eating or overeating. Even if you find your appetite to be non-existent (which is very common during times of stress) try to keep your nutrition game up during difficult times by following these tips

Keep a routine. It might sound obvious to 'eat regularly', but it's really important to eat three square meals a day to ensure you're getting all the nutrients your body and mind needs to function properly. Set meal times that fit your schedule and try your best to stick to them. You might get to your mealtime and feel less than enthusiastic about the chicken rice and broccoli staring back at you, but try to eat it. You'll feel better for it!

Plan ahead. Meal planning might sound boring, but it'll really come in handy when you're in a bad place. Stock up on essentials so you always have things in your pantry that you can turn into a nutritious meal quickly and easily rather than relying on takeout all the time.

Make it easy. The main point here is to work smart not hard, so that might mean buying frozen ready meals that you can prepare easily. An alternative - and definitely healthier option - is to batch cook on days when your energy levels are higher so you can freeze and reheat during low energy times.

Balance is everything. Ideally you want to feed your mind and body the basic things it needs to function (high-quality protein, healthy fats, vitamins, minerals and carbs), but if having that chocolate brownie to look forward to is what gets you through a stressful workday, eat the brownie, King! It's important to include treats in your diet in order to make it sustainable for the long-term.

Use the next page to plan your meals for a full week. Pay attention to any patterns that come up. Does food and drink affect your mood? Do difficult emotions trigger poor food choices?

date:

meal planner

	BREAKFAST	LUNCH	DINNER
MON			
TUE			
WED			
THU			
FRI			
SAT			
SUN			

reflection

What did you learn from planning your meals for a week? Did you learn anything new about your relationship with food? Did you try new recipes? Reflect on your experience here

rest up

Poor mental health usually interferes with our sleep; either sleeping more or less than normal. As a result, sleep difficulties then compound our existing issues. Sleep problems include finding it hard to fall asleep or stay asleep, or not feeling rested during the day. Here are some tips for getting your sleep right

Set a sleep schedule. Setting a standard bed-time and rising time gets your brain and body into a rhythm of consistent sleep. While it might be tempting to reduce your sleep in favor of a late night gaming session or a Netflix binge, try to prioritize getting to sleep at a decent time so you can meet your sleep target every night. Even if it's a weekend, try to wake up within an hour or 2 of your weekday rising time so you don't throw your schedule out of whack.

Create a pre-sleep routine. Now, a nighttime pamper session might not be your thing, but creating some sort of routine you carry out every night before bed can really help you fall asleep easier. Switch off your devices, dim the lights and maybe try guided meditation or deep breathing exercises to put you in the sleep mindset.

Optimize your space. Make sure your sleeping environment is as comfortable as possible. Block out light with heavy curtains or an eye mask, minimize noise with ear plugs and make sure the temperature is right (65 degrees fahrenheit is ideal). If you can, invest in good quality bedding, pillows and a premium mattress for a game-changing night's sleep!

Don't overdo it with alcohol and caffeine. Everyone has their vices, but it's wise to moderate your consumption of these stimulants, especially right before bed. Alcohol might help you fall asleep initially, but it actually decreases overall sleep quality and you're more likely to experience sleep disruptions. As for caffeine, we know it gives us that burst of energy, but over consumption of coffee might actually be masking your poor sleeping habits.

Use the next page to log your sleep for a full week. Keeping a record of your sleep will help you identify what influences your sleep quality and what habits you can introduce or minimize to improve your sleep.

date: _____

sleep log

MON

Went to sleep: _____ Woke up: _____ Undisrupted hours slept: _____

Pre-sleep activity: _____

How I felt the following day: _____

TUE

Went to sleep: _____ Woke up: _____ Undisrupted hours slept: _____

Pre-sleep activity: _____

How I felt the following day: _____

WED

Went to sleep: _____ Woke up: _____ Undisrupted hours slept: _____

Pre-sleep activity: _____

How I felt the following day: _____

THU

Went to sleep: _____ Woke up: _____ Undisrupted hours slept: _____

Pre-sleep activity: _____

How I felt the following day: _____

FRI

Went to sleep: _____ Woke up: _____ Undisrupted hours slept: _____

Pre-sleep activity: _____

How I felt the following day: _____

SAT

Went to sleep: _____ Woke up: _____ Undisrupted hours slept: _____

Pre-sleep activity: _____

How I felt the following day: _____

SUN

Went to sleep: _____ Woke up: _____ Undisrupted hours slept: _____

Pre-sleep activity: _____

How I felt the following day: _____

reflection

What did you learn from tracking your sleep for a full week? What will you implement going forward to optimize your sleep?

goal getter

Goal setting is all about planning for the future and thinking about what you want out of life. Goals are crucial to staying on track and keeping a positive mindset. Here are some tips for setting goals

Visualize. Before setting goals, you should think about what you want your life to look like in the future, who you want to be, and explore your 'why'. The values exercises from p.7 onwards should help with this. Once you've visualized your future, work your way back and identify the goals you need achieve in order to make it your reality. These could be health, career, relationship, financial or community related.

Set SMART goals. You've probably heard of this criteria for goal setting before. It's popular for a reason - because it works! The idea is that you set goals that meet 5 criteria in order to give yourself the best chance of success. The criteria are:
- Specific: You have to be clear about what your aim is. Your goals should specify as many 'who, what, when, where and why's' as relevant. E.g. a specific goal would be: 'I am going to improve my fitness by running for 20 minutes 5 days a week' rather than a basic goal of: 'do more exercise'
- Measurable: Your goals should include some sort of metric to determine if you've met your goal or not
- Achievable: Your goal should stretch your abilities whilst still being in reach so you're not setting yourself up for failure. Don't play yourself
- Realistic: Set goals that make sense within the context of your life and circumstances. How realistic is it to build a million-dollar business within 12 months? Well, it's subjective... But the main thing is to be honest with yourself
- Time-bound: Set a target date that you can work towards. You can also try setting mini deadlines along the way to make sure you stay on track

Talk to others. Seek support from others and include them on your journey to reaching your goals so they can help with motivation and accountability

Take it slow. As ambitious as you might be feeling, don't go from 0 to 100 with goal setting. As mentioned earlier, it's useful to break goals down into mini goals so you don't get overwhelmed and lose momentum. Start with the easier stuff that you can achieve quickly which in turn will motivate you to keep going

Use the next few pages to establish and plan your goals for the future

goal setting

Write down your overall goal and the mini goals you'll use to achieve it. We'll start to add color to the goals over the next few pages

1 overall long term goal you'll work towards over the next few months and years

2 mini goals you'll work towards in the medium-term (next few months) in order to achieve your overall long- term goal

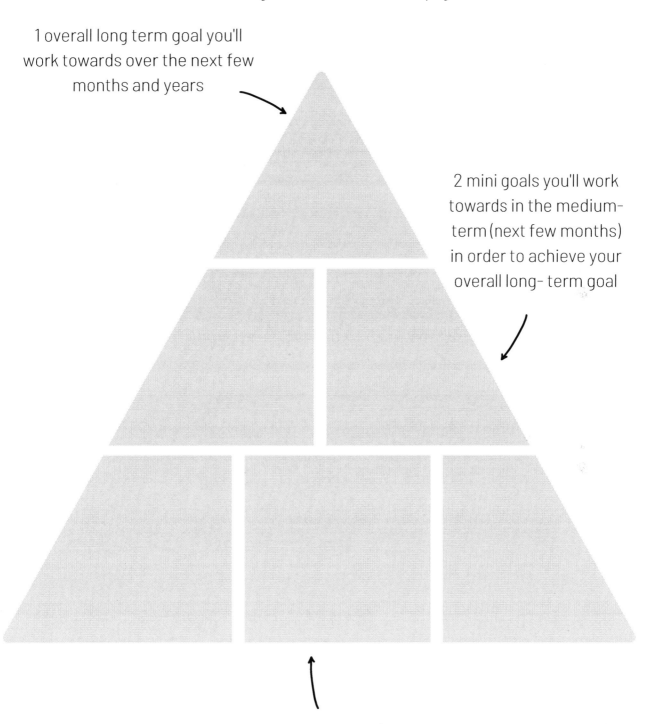

3 mini goals you'll work towards in the short-term (that you can start immediately) in order to achieve your overall long-term goal

goal setting

Create a plan for a long-term goal that you'll work towards over the next year

What is your 1 long term goal?

_____

_____

_____

When will you achieve it by?

_____

Why is this goal important to you and what values underpin it?

_____

_____

_____

_____

_____

_____

_____

If you face obstacles when working on your goal, what will you remind yourself?

_____

_____

_____

_____

goal setting

Create a plan for the 5 medium-short term mini goals you'll take in the next few weeks and months to help you achieve your long-term goal

What are your 2 medium-term mini goals?

1. _____

2. _____

What actions will you take to achieve your goals and when?

_____

_____

_____

_____

_____

What are your 3 short-term mini goals?

1. _____

2. _____

3. _____

What actions will you take to achieve your goals and when?

_____

_____

_____

_____

mental health
assessment

Congratulation on completing the Mental Health Mixtape! As a final step, complete this assessment for the past 2 weeks. How do your answers differ from last time (p.4)? Have you identified any new areas to focus on?

1 = Never   2 = Rarely   3 = Sometimes   4 = Often

	1	2	3	4
I have focused on the things I can control	☐	☐	☐	☐
I have taken time for personal reflection (e.g. journalling)	☐	☐	☐	☐
I have taken a break from social media (2+ hours)	☐	☐	☐	☐
I have attended a counselling / therapy session	☐	☐	☐	☐
I have asked for help if I needed it	☐	☐	☐	☐
I have challenged my negative thoughts	☐	☐	☐	☐
I have taken time to be alone	☐	☐	☐	☐
I have set boundaries with others	☐	☐	☐	☐
I have avoided situations that will trigger me	☐	☐	☐	☐
I have connected with friends and/or family	☐	☐	☐	☐

emergency toolkit

RESOURCES

National Suicide Prevention Lifeline:
Call 1-800-273-8255 (TALK)

National Institute for Mental Health:
www.nimh.nih.gov

Boris L. Henson Foundation Support
Groups:
www.borislhensonfoundation.org

Therapy for Black Men Directory:
www.therapyforblackmen.org

Black Men Heal Mental Health Services:
www.blackmenheal.org

MY SUPPORT SYSTEM

NAME: _____

EMAIL: _____

NUMBER: _____

NAME: _____

EMAIL: _____

NUMBER: _____

NAME: _____

EMAIL: _____

NUMBER: _____

TIPS FOR CHALLENGING TIMES

- <u>Do something that gives you pleasure.</u> Focus on the small pleasures of your day such as your morning coffee or walk in the park. Anything small and achievable will do. Prioritize that moment in your day and spend that time focusing specifically on the feelings of pleasure it gives you

- To combat feelings of powerlessness commonly experienced in challenging times, <u>take action, no matter how small.</u> This could be something like making a doctor's appointment or calling a friend.

- <u>Take time to breathe.</u> Use the exercise provided on p.28 or find a quiet space wherever you are and take ten deep breaths. Repeat this until you feel more grounded and relaxed. This will help you to focus on the here-and-now rather than becoming consumed with negative thoughts

- Refer back to your <u>affirmations</u> on p.41 as a reminder to be kind to yourself

- Refer back to your <u>triggers</u> on p.24 as a reminder of who/what to avoid (if possible) as to not make things worse

templates

Here you'll find templates of some of the exercises from the book if you'd like to do more of them in the future

challenging my negative thoughts

Negative thoughts are normal, but it's important to challenge them so they don't stick. Now we've begun to recognize negative thoughts and styles, we'll develop some strategies to challenge these thoughts. Ask yourself the questions below to interrogate how logical this thinking is

What is the negative thought?

What evidence do you have to support this thought?

What evidence do you have against this thought?

What might you say to a friend who expressed this thought?

Does this negative thought motivate you to change?

If this thought is true, what is the worst case scenario?

challenging my negative thoughts

Negative thoughts are normal, but it's important to challenge them so they don't stick. Now we've begun to recognize negative thoughts and styles, we'll develop some strategies to challenge these thoughts. Ask yourself the questions below to interrogate how logical this thinking is

What is the negative thought?

What evidence do you have to support this thought?

What evidence do you have against this thought?

What might you say to a friend who expressed this thought?

Does this negative thought motivate you to change?

If this thought is true, what is the worst case scenario?

challenging my negative thoughts

Negative thoughts are normal, but it's important to challenge them so they don't stick. Now we've begun to recognize negative thoughts and styles, we'll develop some strategies to challenge these thoughts. Ask yourself the questions below to interrogate how logical this thinking is

What is the negative thought?

What evidence do you have to support this thought?

What evidence do you have against this thought?

What might you say to a friend who expressed this thought?

Does this negative thought motivate you to change?

If this thought is true, what is the worst case scenario?

challenging my negative thoughts

Negative thoughts are normal, but it's important to challenge them so they don't stick. Now we've begun to recognize negative thoughts and styles, we'll develop some strategies to challenge these thoughts. Ask yourself the questions below to interrogate how logical this thinking is

What is the negative thought?

What evidence do you have to support this thought?

What evidence do you have against this thought?

What might you say to a friend who expressed this thought?

Does this negative thought motivate you to change?

If this thought is true, what is the worst case scenario?

challenging my negative thoughts

Negative thoughts are normal, but it's important to challenge them so they don't stick. Now we've begun to recognize negative thoughts and styles, we'll develop some strategies to challenge these thoughts. Ask yourself the questions below to interrogate how logical this thinking is

What is the negative thought?

What evidence do you have to support this thought?

What evidence do you have against this thought?

What might you say to a friend who expressed this thought?

Does this negative thought motivate you to change?

If this thought is true, what is the worst case scenario?

date:

cool off

Now you've learned the skills to effectively identify and manage your emotions, try putting them into practice. The next time you think you've been triggered (and when you're no longer feeling angry or emotional), reflect on the questions below

What happened?
What was the trigger? Describe it below and explain how it came about

_____
_____
_____
_____

What do you feel?
Did you notice a change in your body? What sensations did you feel? Where did your mind go? Write this down

_____
_____
_____
_____

What next?
What were the consequences of your actions as a result of your heightened emotions? What can you do you stay in control of the situation next time? Write your action plan below

_____
_____
_____
_____

cool off

Now you've learned the skills to effectively identify and manage your emotions, try putting them into practice. The next time you think you've been triggered (and when you're no longer feeling angry or emotional), reflect on the questions below

What happened?

What was the trigger? Describe it below and explain how it came about

_____
_____
_____
_____

What do you feel?

Did you notice a change in your body? What sensations did you feel? Where did your mind go? Write this down

_____
_____
_____
_____

What next?

What were the consequences of your actions as a result of your heightened emotions? What can you do you stay in control of the situation next time? Write your action plan below

_____
_____
_____
_____

cool off

Now you've learned the skills to effectively identify and manage your emotions, try putting them into practice. The next time you think you've been triggered (and when you're no longer feeling angry or emotional), reflect on the questions below

What happened?
What was the trigger? Describe it below and explain how it came about

_____
_____
_____
_____

What do you feel?
Did you notice a change in your body? What sensations did you feel? Where did your mind go? Write this down

_____
_____
_____
_____

What next?
What were the consequences of your actions as a result of your heightened emotions? What can you do you stay in control of the situation next time? Write your action plan below

_____
_____
_____
_____

cool off

Now you've learned the skills to effectively identify and manage your emotions, try putting them into practice. The next time you think you've been triggered (and when you're no longer feeling angry or emotional), reflect on the questions below

What happened?   What was the trigger? Describe it below and explain how it came about

_____

_____

_____

_____

What do you feel?   Did you notice a change in your body? What sensations did you feel? Where did your mind go? Write this down

_____

_____

_____

_____

What next?   What were the consequences of your actions as a result of your heightened emotions? What can you do you stay in control of the situation next time? Write your action plan below

_____

_____

_____

_____

cool off

Now you've learned the skills to effectively identify and manage your emotions, try putting them into practice. The next time you think you've been triggered (and when you're no longer feeling angry or emotional), reflect on the questions below

What happened?   What was the trigger? Describe it below and explain how it came about

_____

_____

_____

_____

What do you feel?   Did you notice a change in your body? What sensations did you feel? Where did your mind go? Write this down

_____

_____

_____

_____

What were the consequences of your actions as a result of your **What next?** heightened emotions? What can you do you stay in control of the situation next time? Write your action plan below

_____

_____

_____

_____

date:

meal planner

	BREAKFAST	LUNCH	DINNER
MON			
TUE			
WED			
THU			
FRI			
SAT			
SUN			

meal planner

	BREAKFAST	LUNCH	DINNER
MON			
TUE			
WED			
THU			
FRI			
SAT			
SUN			

date:

meal planner

	BREAKFAST	LUNCH	DINNER
MON			
TUE			
WED			
THU			
FRI			
SAT			
SUN			

date:

meal planner

	BREAKFAST	LUNCH	DINNER
MON			
TUE			
WED			
THU			
FRI			
SAT			
SUN			

date:

meal planner

	BREAKFAST	LUNCH	DINNER
MON			
TUE			
WED			
THU			
FRI			
SAT			
SUN			

exercise planner

	WEEK 1	WEEK 2	WEEK 3	WEEK 4	WEEK 5
MON					
TUE					
WED					
THU					
FRI					
SAT					
SUN					

exercise planner

	WEEK 1	WEEK 2	WEEK 3	WEEK 4	WEEK 5
MON					
TUE					
WED					
THU					
FRI					
SAT					
SUN					

date:

exercise planner

	WEEK 1	WEEK 2	WEEK 3	WEEK 4	WEEK 5
MON					
TUE					
WED					
THU					
FRI					
SAT					
SUN					

exercise planner

	WEEK 1	WEEK 2	WEEK 3	WEEK 4	WEEK 5
MON					
TUE					
WED					
THU					
FRI					
SAT					
SUN					

exercise planner

	WEEK 1	WEEK 2	WEEK 3	WEEK 4	WEEK 5
MON					
TUE					
WED					
THU					
FRI					
SAT					
SUN					

notes

notes

notes

notes

notes

notes

notes

notes

notes

date:

notes

notes

notes

notes

notes

notes

notes

notes

notes

date:

notes

notes

How was it for you?

We hope this book was valuable for you. If you did gain something from it, please consider supporting us by leaving a review on Amazon

Gift one of our other books to a Black woman in your life!

SELF CARE WORKBOOK FOR BLACK WOMEN
A 150+ page activity book covering mental, physical, spiritual and emotional self help practices. Complete with a 12-month planner and guided journal

SPIRITUAL SELF CARE FOR BLACK WOMEN
A guided journal and 12-month planner with more in-depth self reflection and spirituality activities

EMOTIONAL SELF CARE FOR BLACK WOMEN
A self help activity book and guided journal to specifically address the thoughts, beliefs and triggers which affect your emotions and behavior

PRAYER JOURNAL FOR BLACK WOMEN
52 Week Devotional with bible verses, gratitude checklists, lessons from God, prayers for others

Printed in Great Britain
by Amazon

36909715R10068